On a Bed of Oyster Shells I Stand

The Vital and Complex Story of York's Black Oyster Culture

FRIENDS OF LEBANON CEMETERY

Copyright © 2023 by Friends of Lebanon Cemetery

All rights reserved.

No portion of this book may be reproduced in any form without written permission from the publisher or author, except as permitted by U.S. copyright law.

The Friends of Lebanon Cemetery assumes no responsibility of references and notes contained herein. This publication has been produced using funds from Friends of Lebanon Cemetery, York, Pennsylvania.

Information compiled by Tina Charles, Jenny DeJesus Marshall, Rebecca Anstine and Samantha Dorm. Written by Tina Charles.

Contents

Introduction — 1

Background — 3

Oystering Origins — 7
    The Other Underground Railroad

Oyster Cellars, Saloons and Restaurants — 11
    Stephen Davidge
    Gabriel Butler
    Hamilton and Thomas Gray

Oyster Peddlers — 19
    John Reeves
    Lewis Woodyard
    George (Joseph) McIntosh

The Black Oyster Culture Today — 23

Oyster Recipes 25
   1902
   1909
   1928
   1935
   1967

Endnotes 32

Introduction

Every October since 1974, the York County History Center has celebrated York's Colonial heritage by hosting an Oyster Festival in downtown York. The idea behind this fundraising event came from the discovery of oyster shells during an archeological dig behind the Golden Plough Tavern in the 1960s.

Oyster festivals have become gatherings where stories are shared, traditions are celebrated, and the flavors of the past blend seamlessly with the present. Old York newspaper articles tell a story that both the elite and the blue collar worker could dine on these creatures in oyster cellars, pubs, restaurants, and at home thanks to oyster peddlers who pushed their carts around the city.

At the Oyster Festival, many thoughts go through our minds about how to eat them – raw, fried, broiled, grilled, stewed, on a sandwich. But rarely does the history cross our minds that led up to this point, especially the fact that Black people have been harvesting, cultivating, and selling these bivalves since at least the 18th century.

We have "dredged up" a few of York's Black oyster entrepreneurs of the 19th century. These rare pearls expand on York's Oyster Culture. Are you ready to dive in and help us celebrate the cultural significance of oysters the hearts and minds of York's community?

BACKGROUND

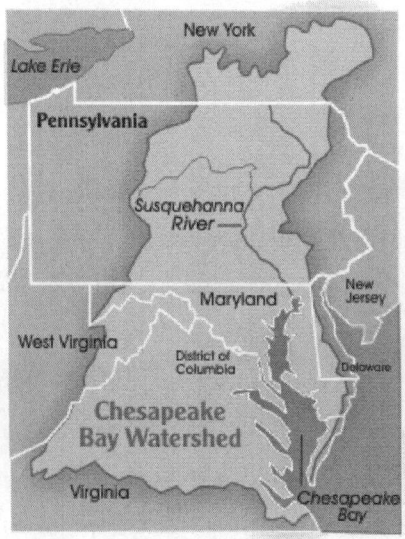

YORK, PENNSYLVANIA IS NOT considered to "sit" on water, as the Codorus Creek and the Susquehanna River don't count. However, both of these tributaries empty into the Chesapeake

Bay. York is well-connected to Baltimore, and have always had ample access to "the bounty of the Bay," so to speak.

Throughout history, oysters have been revered as symbols of connection. For Black people, they carry an even deeper meaning – a testament to resilience and a celebration of cultural heritage.

The Oyster

Oysters have been around for over 15 million years. They are members of the bivalve mollusk family (along with clams, scallops, and mussels). They are easily identified by their non-symmetrical shells, their fascinating ability to form pearls, and as vacuum cleaners of the bays for their ability to filter the water. Long before any explorers stepped foot onto the East Coast, oysters paved the bottom of the sea all along the coastline. Oysters were able to successfully "reef" or build on each other's shells to create massive colonies that ran hundreds of miles up and down the coast.

Susquehanna River & Chesapeake Bay

The mighty Susquehanna is one of the oldest rivers in the world. It is the nation's 16th largest river and the largest river lying entirely in the United States that flows into the Atlantic Ocean. The river meanders 444 miles from its origin in Otsego Lake near Cooperstown, NY until it empties into the Chesapeake Bay at Havre de Grace, MD. The name Susquehanna is a name derived from the Delaware Indian name "Sisa'we'had'hanna" which means *River Oyster*.

The Chesapeake Bay is justifiably famous for its oysters. One translation of the word Chesapeake from the Algonquian Indian language is "Great Shellfish Bay." The bay had virtually ideal conditions for oysters. Ocean water from the Atlantic was diluted by fresh water flowing into the Chesapeake to produce the moderately salty (brackish) water in which oysters thrive.

In the early 17th century, Captain John Smith described oysters lying "as thick as stones." Oysters were so abundant that their reefs neared the water's surface, sometimes becoming navigational hazards for ships. By the end of the 19th century, it was estimated that more than 15 million bushels of oysters were being harvested annually from the Maryland portion of the Bay. According to a study by the Chesapeake Biological Laboratory, by 2011, the oyster population in the upper Chesapeake Bay was estimated to be 0.3 percent of population levels of early 1800s due to overfishing, habitat loss, and disease.

DID YOU KNOW?

Oyster shells are recyclable! You can return your shells at several drop off locations around the Chesapeake Bay, and they'll be reused to help grow juvenile oysters.

Oystering Origins

Oysters have long sustained black folks in the Chesapeake area. Black people have played a role in the waterways since the founding of the states that make up the Chesapeake region. The Chesapeake Bay was both an entry-point to slavery in North America and a gateway to freedom and opportunity. Enslaved Africans brought to the Americas with them many ancient skills they developed from working on the water, including oystering, crabbing, boat-building and net-making. And in 1796, long before the passage of the Emancipation Proclamation, the federal government began issuing Seamen's Protection Certificates, which defined those who held them as American citizens. This allowed Black men, also known as "Black Jacks" to work alongside White men as equals on the water. By 1803 about 18 percent of America's seafaring jobs were freed Blacks, filling every type of job in the industry.

By the 1820s, most registered oystermen were African American, and opportunity in the industry was abundant, especially for York's Black community, who came from oyster-rich states along the Chesapeake Bay like Maryland and Virginia.

The Other Underground Railroad

"Chesapeake Station"

Most Americans are familiar with the Underground Railroad and Harriet Tubman, a conductor of the Underground Railroad who returned to the south over nineteen times to help enslaved Black people to freedom. What is not as well known is that Tubman led these folks to freedom using the Chesapeake Bay. A significant portion of the Underground Railroad took place on water. The Bay and its rivers were referred to as the Chesapeake Station or Chesapeake Underground. The Chesapeake Bay's waterways were pathways to freedom.

Fugitives escaped using the Bay's waterways by sneaking onto docked vessels that would take them up the Bay and into the Susquehanna River, receiving assistance from ship captains that would allow them to board their ships, and crossing the Potomac River. Although it's difficult to know the exact routes that freedom seekers followed, many used the collection of nautical charts known as the U.S. Coast Survey, created in 1807. It identified the shoreline, water depths, and navigation hazards. Abolitionists and African Americans, both freed and enslaved, became very familiar with this piece of information to help navigate the eastern coast.

Runaways depended on maritime blacks. Their maritime culture provided a complex system of informants, messengers, go-betweens and other collaborators. Even Frederick Douglass used the common presence of Black watermen to his advantage. Douglass attempted escape via the Chesapeake Bay and wrote in his autobiography, "Our reason for taking the water route was, that we were less liable to be suspected as runaways; we hoped to be regarded as fishermen."

Douglass's attempt to escape by canoeing up the Bay and into Pennsylvania was unsuccessful. After this first attempt, he was sent to work in Baltimore's shipyards. Douglass eventually escaped slavery via a train from Baltimore to Philadelphia. He disguised himself as a free Black sailor and borrowed a friend's Seaman's Protection Certificate, which served as his free papers.

York's Black citizens were very involved in the Underground Railroad. Using the close proximity to Baltimore via the rivers and Bay, this gave York's Black oyster vendors the perfect scenario to help freedom seekers.

Oyster Cellars, Saloons and Restaurants

Oysters, Strawberries, and Ice Cream

From the early 1800s through the Civil War, York's Black citizens were owners of some of the most frequented oyster cellars and saloons.[1]

Stephen Davidge

One of the earliest mentions of an oyster cellar found was that of Stephen Davidge (also spelled Davage and Davige), who advertised in the Pennsylvania Republican that he has moved his oyster cellar back into the apartment next to the office of George Haller, Esq. with an entrance from the alley immediately opposite the public offices. Mr. Davidge was born around 1794 in Maryland. He was a very well-known barber, owning several barbershops around town. From the early 1800s until around 1850, he also was the owner of oyster cellars close to the center square of the city. This was a perfect business for a man involved in the Underground Railroad; helping to hide runaways in his oyster cellars, much like New York's famed Oyster King, Thomas Downing. Mr. Davidge was also one of the founders of the African Methodist Episcopal Zion church in 1819, which was located in the 100 block of North Duke Street and was also known to be involved with the Underground Railroad.

> **Oysters! Oysters!**
> **Stephen Davidge,**
> Returns his most sincere thanks to his customers for past favors, and informs them and the public that he has removed, and opened an oyster cellar under the house of John Koons, innkeeper in Mainstreet, near the Market House; where gentlemen giving him a call will be waited on in the best style, and have oysters expeditiously served up in all the various ways that may be desired—
> With broiled and stewed and toasted,
> With fried and baked and roasted,
> He treats the town—
> And country too—and hopes, by his attention and endeavors to please, to merit a continuance of past favors.
> York, Jan. 16, 1821.

An 1821 advertisement notified his patrons that he was moving his location to Main Street, near the Market House (which was located in the center of the square downtown). What is an oyster "cellar"? These were often located in the basement of establishments where keeping ice was easier. As the ad declared, Davidge kept his "oyster cellar" under Mr. Koon's inn at that time.

Twenty years later, in 1847, we see another advertisement that he fit up a room in his home on West Philadelphia Street, between North George and North Beaver streets, *"where he will be prepared at all times to accommodate those who may be disposed to encourage him with the very best Oysters that the Baltimore Market can produce ... "*.

> **OYSTERS!**
> **NEW ESTABLISHMENT.**
> STEPHEN DAVIGE respectfully informs the public that he has fitted up a room in his dwelling, in West Philadelphia St., between George and Beaver Streets, where he will be prepared at all times to accommodate those who may be disposed to encourage him with the very best Oysters that the Baltimore Market can produce, *STEWED, FRIED, ROASTED OR IN THE SHELL.*
> ☞ *Private Families* will be supplied at all times with Oysters of the best quality.
> S. D. hopes by strict attention to business and a determination to accommodate, to receive the favor of the public.
> York, February 10, 1847.   3w

Gabriel Butler

In 1850, listings in newspapers for Maryland-born Gabriel Butler as a "Beer and Oyster House" entrepreneur started showing up. Little is known about Mr. Butler because his time in York was brief.

Establishments serving oysters went by various names, especially when paired with beer in a bar-like setting. Oysters were seen as a cheap food to accompany beer and liquor so a person could find both in oyster bars, oyster parlors, oyster saloons, or oyster cellars. From 1851 through 1855, Gabriel was listed in the newspapers under "Vendors of Oysters and Ale in York". By 1851, he was joined in those listings by the Gray family.

Hamilton and Thomas Gray

The Gray (also spelled Grey) family is believed to have migrated to York from Maryland. Their home was also located in the 100 block of North Duke Street with the A .M.E. Zion church and the family was also heavily involved in the Underground Railroad, having connections to the Jakes family in Baltimore, Maryland. Throughout the 1850s, Hamilton and Thomas Gray were noted to run oyster cellars. This was around the same time that Mr. Butler opened his business.

In an 1851 estate sale listing for the property of Jacob Bomgardner in the York Gazette, there was a 2-½ story frame and rough-cast house on the same property occupied by Thomas Gray as an oyster 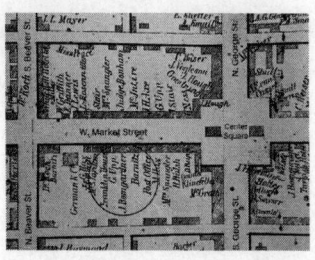 house. The property adjoined the property of C.A. Barnitz and George Upp, Jr. An 1850 map of York City shows this location in the first block from the square on West Market Street (within circle).

In 1852, Thomas Gray was listed in the People's Advocate as having an "oyster and ice cream saloon".

According to an 1853 ad, Thomas Gray opened a restaurant at his residence. located "on the hill opposite the Presbyterian church." *He will be prepared to furnish in season, upon the most reasonable terms,* **OYSTERS, STRAWBERRIES, ICE CREAM & C.** He stated he would keep it open all year and guaranteed an *abundant supply of fresh, rich and unadulterated cream.*

In 1854, Thomas Gray was listed with Gabriel Butler under "Beer Houses, Eating Houses, and Oyster Cellars" in York Borough, 8th class.

In 1855, both Thomas and Hamilton Gray, along with William Butler were listed under "Beer Houses, Eating Houses, Oyster Cellars, & c." in York Borough – 8th class. Between 1856-1859, only Hamilton Gray was listed under "Oysters" on the retailers list in the newspapers.

Oyster Peddlers

After the Civil War ended, Black oystermen continued to dominate the industry. By 1860, the Chesapeake Bay was the main supplier of oysters in the United States. The availability of jobs and the expansion of railroads and steamships led many Black men to the region to work in the oyster industry. York's Black citizens transitioned from owning oyster cellars and saloons to peddling oysters and oyster sandwiches from carts throughout the city as a means to help support their families.

John Reeves

> A native of Bryantown, Charles county, Md., Mr. Reeves moved to York in November, 1872. He became connected with the A. M. E. Zion church in 1874 and was one of its most active members in church and Sunday school work. He was a steward of the congregation, a class leader in the Sunday school, and also treasurer of the Sunday school. For a period of thirty-one years he was employed at the National house. Mr. Reeves is believed to be the only colored man in York who wrote an autobiography of his life. Following the severance of his employment at the National house Mr. Reeves entered into business for himself. Until about seven years ago he was a street salesman in oyster sandwiches and crab cakes. He has been living retired. On August 1, 1873, he was chosen as the most popular colored man in York in a contest conducted by the Laurel Fire company. As a prize for this honor he was awarded a gold-headed cane.

Mr. John Reeves was a native of Bryantown, Charles County, Maryland, John and his brother, Thomas Reeves, came to York in 1872. Charles County is located in southern Maryland and is bordered by the Potomac and Patuxent rivers. In 1873, he was voted the most popular colored man in York.

John worked as a porter for the National House for over 30 years, after which he went into business for himself as a very successful caterer and street vendor of oyster sandwiches and seafood. Mr. Reeves was so successful in his business that he was able to purchase homes for all of his children, including his well-known daughter, Helen Reeves-Thackston, for whom Thackston Park in York City is named.

Lewis Woodyard

Born in 1897 in Maryland, Lewis migrated to York with his family between 1900 and 1902. At the age of 18, Lewis owned an oyster cart and peddled oyster sandwiches. The *York Daily* reported 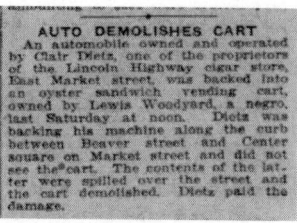 in 1915 Lewis brought charges against two men who stole oyster sandwiches amongst other things from his cart that he had left out front of the infamous Lafayette Club while he went to a nearby pool room to get a few rounds in. Then in 1916, his oyster cart was hit by a car and demolished.

George (Joseph) McIntosh

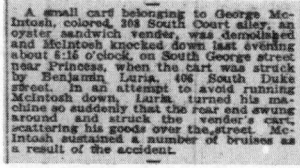 George McIntosh was born in 1881. He was noted to hold several jobs over the years, working as a waiter at the Hotel Penn, as a garbage collector in 1903, and having his own barbershop in 1906. He also owned an oyster

cart. An article in the *York Dispatch* in 1916 described George McIntosh's oyster cart being knocked down, scattering his goods all over the street.

The Black Oyster Culture Today

The oystering craft is still practiced by descendants of those oystermen who found their livelihood on the Chesapeake Bay long ago. Younger generations are breathing new life into the industry. Inspired by those who came before them, this new generation of Black oyster entrepreneurs are reclaiming their rightful place in the industry with oyster farming, opening oyster bars and restaurants, and holding oyster festivals. More importantly, they are sharing their family histories, and the struggles and triumphs of African Americans and their strong ties to the oyster industry. They are strong advocates for conservation, creating nonprofit organizations and partnering with their local, state and federal conservancy agencies.

So as you enjoy those oysters at the York Oyster Festival, please take a moment to reflect on the history and remember the names and stories of these remarkable individuals. Their legacy lives on in each oyster, reminding us of the indomitable spirit and unwavering determination of Black Americans who, against all odds, carved a place for themselves in the oyster industry.

To learn more about and/or support Black oyster culture, visit the following websites:

Blacks of the Chesapeake https://blacksofthechesapeake.wildapricot.org/

Black Men, Blue Waters https://www.mdsg.umd.edu/sites/default/files/files/MN16_2_BlackMenBlueWaters.PDF

Waterbound https://storymaps.arcgis.com/stories/1c6f8f445a7c43e5982e6e4682df537e

Minorities in Aquaculture https://www.mianpo.org/

Black Girls Dive https://blackgirlsdivefoundation.org/

OYSTER RECIPES

OYSTERS HAVE ALWAYS BEEN very popular in York and there was no shortage of recipes shared in newspapers. In 1877, an article on "Oyster Stew" made some bold claims:[2]

This is the season for Oysters and York is the place, in our opinion, where you can get the best "done up" stew, fry, roast or chafe in the "seven States." When we say "seven States," it means that we have eaten oysters in that many "Members" in the "galaxy of this Union" but have yet to see the place that can beat good Old York in the preparation and serving up of this delicious bivalve. The fact is that here the flavor of the oyster is not destroyed by too many other admixtures – all our caterers want to make them rich and palatable, is good sweet butter and salt, if needed. When a man has a love for oysters – wants to eat oysters and taste the oyster while eating he don't want the dish to be made up with flour, milk, eggs and "what not" – he wants oysters, and know, while eating, that he is actually tasting them. To contrast the York style with the different "improved" styles prevailing elsewhere, read the following.

> With a little of liquor, or milk, mix smoothly about a tablespoon of butter and half a tablespoon of flour (do not let it be lumpy). Warm about a cupful of milk (with a scrap of maces if you like, or a grate of nutmeg), stir into this the butter and flour - have it quite smooth - be sure to stir always one way, or it will curdle. Now add your oysters, put the pan on the fire, and when it comes up to a boil, if the oysters are "plumped up," your stew is ready.

1902

An advertisement from The Natural Food Company in Niagara Falls, maker of Shredded Whole Wheat Biscuit. *It wholly nourishes the whole body. It is most appetizing as toast. It can be combined with all kinds of vegetables, meats or delicacies and makes healthful as well as delicious dishes.* Here is one of many combinations:

A Seasonal Recipe for Creamed Oysters in Baskets of Shredded Whole Wheat Biscuit

Prepare 5 Shredded Whole Wheat Biscuits by cutting with a sharp pointed knife an oblong cavity from the top of the Biscuit 1/4 inch from sides and ends. Remove the top and all inside shreds, forming a basket. Dust these lightly with celery salt and paprika and heat through while you are preparing the 1 pint of oysters. Remove all bits of shell. Prepare a sauce by blending in the blazer 1-1/2 tablespoons butter, 1-1/2 tablespoons Entire Wheat flour, 1/2 teaspoon salt and 1/8 teaspoon paprika, then add 1 cup milk and 1/2 cup cream and stir until thick and smooth, then cook the oysters until plump, add to the sauce and fill the Biscuit baskets. Serve at once.[3]

1909

Oyster Sausage

Scald two dozen large oysters in their own liquor and when they are cool chop fine. Mix with them 5 ounces of bread crumbs and 3 ounces of finely chopped suet. Season with salt, pepper and a grating of nutmeg. Stir in a beaten egg and set away for an hour or two to cool and get firm. Flour the hands and make up into sausage cakes and fry them in butter or hot olive oil. Serve with tender celery and brown bread and butter.[4]

Oysters on a Strip of Toast

Toast oblong strips of bread on one side only. On the untoasted side of each put two large, fat, broiled oysters. Melt a tablespoon of butter in a sauce pain, add two tablespoonfuls of grated cheese and stir until smooth. Then stir into the mixture the yolk of one egg beaten with a little cream. Season with salt and tabasco and stir until smooth. Remove from the fire and pour a little of the sauce over each oyster. Serve with rings of lemon.[5]

Oyster Loaf

Cut the top crust from a long, thin loaf of stale bread and with a spoon scoop out the inside, leaving the walls smooth. Brown 2 tablespoons of butter in a saucepan, add a half teaspoonful of grated onion and half teaspoon of finely chopped parsley. Season with salt and pepper and brown again. Stir in a tablespoon of flour, add the strained liquor from a quart of oysters and boil. Fill the loaf with the uncooked oysters, seasoning with salt, pepper and little finely-minced celery. Put generous amount of butter over the top and replace the crust. Put in a baking pan and pour over the loaf part of the sauce. Bake about 30 minutes, basting occasionally with the remainder of the sauce.[6]

Oyster Scones

Peel and boil five medium-sized potatoes. Drain and mash them, seasoning with salt, pepper and 2 tablespoons of butter. Whip with a wire egg beater until light and creamy. Mix in 1 pint of oysters and turn out on a floured board. Roll out a half inch thick and cut with a biscuit cutter. Brush with melted butter and dip in beaten egg seasoned with salt and pepper. Fry on a griddle greased with hot olive oil or butter. Have both sides golden brown.[7]

1928

Deviled Oysters

Put 1 pint minced oysters in saucepan with 1 tablespoon melted butter and 1/4 pint cream. Season with salt and pepper and add 1/2 cup cracker crumbs. Simmer 5 minutes, stirring gently. Put in a baking dish, sprinkle 1/2 cup bread crumbs and bits of butter over top. Bake until top is a rich golden brown in very hot oven. Serves four.[8]

Panned Oysters

Put 2 tablespoons butter in saucepan, when hot add 1 pint oysters. Cook until edges begin to curl, then add 1/2 cup cream, salt and pepper. Serves four.[9]

Scalloped Oysters

Put 1 quart oysters (strain and reserve liquor) in layers in baking dish, alternating with bread or cracker crumbs, bits of butter and season to taste with salt and pepper. When dish is filled add strained oyster liquor and sufficient milk to moisten. Cover with crumbs and 1 tablespoon of butter in bits. Bake 30 minutes in hot oven. Serves six.[10]

1935

Strickler's offered a series of oyster recipes for free with each purchase of a pint can.

OYSTER RECIPES

1967

Chincoteague Oysters

Use 1 pint oysters, drained and chopped. Mix together and sift 2 cups flour, 3 teaspoons baking powder, 1 teaspoon salt, pepper (if desired). Beat 2 eggs and add 1 cup milk, 1 tablespoon Crisco oil. Blend dry ingredients with egg mixture to form smooth batter. Add oysters and drop by teaspoon into hot fat for about 3 minutes.[11]

1. Image Credit: Library Company of Philadelphia. *Philadelphia Taste Displayed. Or, bon-ton below stairs.* Drawn on stone by James Akin.

2. *The York Daily,* 01 Dec 1877, p.4

3. *The York Dispatch,* 01 Nov 1902, p.3

4. *The York Daily,* 06 Nov 1909, p.5

5. *The York Daily,* 06 Nov 1909, p.5

6. *The York Daily,* 06 Nov 1909, p.5

7. *The York Daily,* 06 Nov 1909, p.5

8. *York Daily Record,* 19 Dec 1928, p.12

9. *York Daily Record,* 19 Dec 1928, p.12

10. *York Daily Record,* 19 Dec 1928, p.12

11. *York Daily Record,* 09 Jun 1967, p.14

Made in the USA
Middletown, DE
29 December 2024